THE ISIDORE & FAY RUDIN
CHILDREN'S LITERATURE COLLECTION
established June, 1995
The Jewish Education Center of Cleveland

*Funded by the Isidore & Fay Rudin Fund of
The Jewish Community Federation of Cleveland*

```
RMC      Rosinsky, Natalie M.
244.1    Hanukkah
ROS

15715
```

Hanukkah

RATNER MEDIA AND TECHNOLOGY CENTER
JEWISH EDUCATION CENTER OF CLEVELAND

by Natalie M. Rosinsky

Content Adviser: Ina Regosin, Dean of Students, Hebrew College,
Newton Centre, Massachusetts

Reading Adviser: Dr. Linda D. Labbo, Department of Reading Education,
College of Education, The University of Georgia

Let's See Library
Compass Point Books
Minneapolis, Minnesota

Compass Point Books
3722 West 50th Street, #115
Minneapolis, MN 55410

Visit Compass Point Books on the Internet at *www.compasspointbooks.com* or e-mail your request to *custserv@compasspointbooks.com*

Cover: Menorah lit for Hanukkah

Photographs ©: Richard T. Nowitz, cover, 12, 16; Richard T. Nowitz/Corbis, 4, 20; Bettmann/Corbis, 6; Dave Bartruff/Corbis, 8; Ted Spiegel/Corbis, 10; Photri-Microstock, 14; Mark Thiessen/Corbis, 18; John Cross/The Free Press, 24.

Editor: Catherine Neitge
Photo Researcher: Svetlana Zhurkina
Photo Selector: Catherine Neitge
Designer: Melissa Voda

Library of Congress Cataloging-in-Publication Data
Rosinsky, Natalie M. (Natalie Myra)
  Hanukkah / by Natalie M. Rosinsky.
    p. cm.— (Let's see library. Holidays)
  Summary: Provides information on the origin of Jewish feast of Hanukkah and some of the ways in which it is celebrated.
  Includes bibliographical references and index.
  ISBN 0-7565-0390-6 (hc)
  1. Hanukkah—Juvenile literature. [1. Hanukkah. 2. Holidays.] I. Title. II. Series.
  BM695.H3 R6125 2002
  296.4'35—dc21   2002003042

© 2003 by Compass Point Books
All rights reserved. No part of this book may be reproduced without written permission from the publisher. The publisher takes no responsibility for the use of any of the materials or methods described in this book, nor for the products thereof.
Printed in the United States of America.

Table of Contents

What Is Hanukkah? 5
How Did Hanukkah Begin? 7
What Is Most Important at Hanukkah? 9
What Are Special Hanukkah Foods? 11
What Is a Hanukkah Game? 13
How Else Is Hanukkah Observed? 15
How Has Hanukkah Changed? 17
How Is Hanukkah Observed in the United States? 19
How Is Hanukkah Observed in Israel? 21
Glossary 22
Did You Know? 22
Want to Know More? 23
Index 24

What Is Hanukkah?

Hanukkah is a happy holiday. It has lights, tasty treats, games, and songs. It is one of the holidays of the Jewish religion. Hanukkah lasts eight days. It takes place every November or December. The dates each year depend on the Jewish calendar.

During Hanukkah, Jews remember winning an important war. This struggle happened more than 2,000 years ago. Jews fought to save their religion. They won the freedom to practice their beliefs. Hanukkah means **"dedication"** in the **Hebrew** language. Sometimes, Hanukkah is also called the Festival of Lights.

◄ *Israeli children celebrate Hanukkah at a Jerusalem school.*

How Did Hanukkah Begin?

In what is now Israel, a king tried to end Judaism. His army killed Jews who prayed together. This king would not allow Jews to read their holy books. He destroyed much of the biggest Jewish **Temple**. Jews fought back. A man named Judah led fighters called the **Maccabees**. They won.

Jews wanted to light their grand Temple's lamp. They only found enough pure oil to burn for one day, though. It would take eight days to make more. What a wonderful surprise! The flame in the Temple lamp burned for eight days! Its light was as strong as the Jews' faith.

◀ *Judah Maccabee leads his fighters against the king's army.*

What Is Most Important at Hanukkah?

Jews light a special lamp each night of Hanukkah. One candle is lit at sundown on the first night. Two candles are lit on the second. Another candle is added every night. At last, eight candles with their "helper" candle glow in the **menorah**. Short Hebrew prayers are said. The menorah is a sign of how strong Judaism is.

Menorahs are lit at home. Family members take turns lighting candles. Sometimes, each person has a menorah.

◀ *Family members gather to light the menorah.*

What Are Special Hanukkah Foods?

Foods cooked in oil are special at Hanukkah. They remind Jews of the oil in the Temple lamp.

Potato pancakes called latkes taste great! Many families put applesauce on top of their latkes (pronounced LOT-kas).

Chocolate coins are also eaten at Hanukkah. They are very popular with children! This **gelt** reminds Jews of their fight against the evil king. His picture had been on real coins. The Jews made new coins with pictures of menorahs or Judah Maccabee.

◄ *A chocolate coin wrapped in gold foil is called gelt.*

What Is a Special Hanukkah Game?

Jews spin a four-sided top called a dreidel at Hanukkah. This dreidel (pronounced DRAY-dl) is part of a game. Each side has a different Hebrew letter. When the dreidel stops, the letter that faces up is important. It tells the spinner whether to take or give back gelt.

Dreidels remind Jews of how they tricked the evil king. They hid their prayers and meetings. When soldiers came by, Jews would pretend to play with tops!

The letters on a dreidel mean "A Great **Miracle** Happened There."

◀ *Children play a Hanukkah game with a dreidel.*

How Else Is Hanukkah Observed?

Family members give each other small gifts. Gelt is often a gift at Hanukkah. Some families give children one small present each night of Hanukkah.

Families sing special songs on this holiday. The song "Rock of Ages" is about having faith. The song "I Have a Little Dreidel" is about having fun!

◄ *Family members sing together during Hanukkah.*

How Has Hanukkah Changed?

The first menorahs were made of stone or clay. Later, metals like brass, iron or silver were used. Early menorahs were simple. Later, fancy menorahs were made to decorate Jewish homes.

The first menorahs burned oil. Later ones burned candles. Many today still use candles, but there are also electric menorahs. Some menorahs are made just for children. These are decorated with cartoon characters, animals, or sports objects.

The first menorahs were placed outside of houses. Today, menorahs are displayed in windows as signs of faith.

◄ A boy lights a menorah.

How Is Hanukkah Observed in the United States?

Hanukkah is observed across the United States. Cities with many Jews often display large menorahs in streets or parks. In New York City's Central Park, the menorah is thirty-two feet (ten meters) tall. In Washington, D.C., the national menorah outside the White House is thirty feet (nine meters) tall.

    Hanukkah is not a national holiday. Schools, businesses, and government offices are open. Most Jewish families gather to light the menorah. They sing songs, play dreidel, and eat latkes. It is a time to be proud of being Jewish.

◀ *A Hanukkah menorah glows near the White House.*

How Is Hanukkah Observed in Israel?

Hanukkah is a national holiday in Israel. Schools, government offices, and businesses are closed. Instead of latkes, children enjoy eating fried doughnuts. Their dreidels are also different in a special way. They have letters meaning "A Great Miracle Happened HERE."

A special fire is lit near the hometown of Judah Maccabee. Runners carry flames from this fire to large cities. Then, they use these flames to light large, outside menorahs.

◀ *A giant Hanukkah menorah is lit in Jerusalem.*

Glossary

dedication—believing in something; devotion to a cause

gelt—money given as gifts on Hanukkah, or chocolate coins, often wrapped in shiny paper

Hebrew—the language Jews speak in Israel and all Jews use in prayers

Maccabee—the Hebrew word for "hammer," used to describe Jewish fighters who "hammered" at the king's army

menorah—lamp holding nine lights at Hanukkah (and seven lights at other times)

miracle—an act that people believe is caused by God

Temple—the main Jewish house of prayer in ancient times, located in Jerusalem

Did You Know?

- There are at least sixteen ways to spell Hanukkah in English. Some of these are Chanukah, Hannukah, and Chanuka.
- The world's tallest menorah is in Israel. This menorah is sixty feet (eighteen meters) high.

Want to Know More?

In the Library
Kimmelman, Leslie. *Dance, Sing, Remember: A Celebration of Jewish Holidays*. New York: HarperCollins, 2000.
Manushkin, Fran. *Latkes and Applesauce*. New York: Scholastic, 1990.
Simon, Norma. *The Story of Hanukkah*. New York: HarperCollins, 1997.

On the Web
Not Just for Kids: Hanukkah
http://www.night.net/kids/hanukkah.html-ssi
To find songs, recipes, and rules for playing dreidel

Billy Bear's Playground
http://www.billybear4kids.com/holidays/hanukkah/hanukkah.htm
For fun activities and games related to Hanukkah

Through the Mail
National Museum of American Jewish History
55 North Fifth Street
Philadelphia, PA 19106
To find out more about Jews and Jewish holidays in America

On the Road
The Jewish Museum
1109 Fifth Avenue
New York, NY 10128
212/423-3200

Spertus Museum
of the Spertus Institute of Jewish Studies
618 South Michigan Avenue
Chicago, IL 60605
312/322-1747
To see menorahs and dreidels from around the world at these two museums

Index

applesauce, 11
candles, 9, 17
Central Park, 19
chocolate coins, 11
dreidels, 13, 19, 21
electric menorahs, 17
Festival of Lights, 5
foods, 11, 19, 21
games, 13, 19
gelt, 11, 13, 15
gifts, 15
Hebrew language, 5, 9, 13
"helper" candle, 9
"I Have a Little Dreidel" song, 15

Israel, 7, 21
Jewish calendar, 5
latkes, 11, 19
Maccabee, Judah, 7, 11, 21
Maccabees, 7
menorahs, 9, 11, 17, 19, 21
New York City, 19
oil, 7, 11, 17
potato pancakes, 11, 19
"Rock of Ages" song, 15
songs, 15, 19
Temple lamp, 7
White House, 19

About the Author
Natalie M. Rosinsky writes about history, science, and other fun things. One of her two cats usually sits on her computer as she works in Mankato, Minnesota. Both cats pay close attention as she and her family make and eat special holiday foods. Natalie earned graduate degrees from the University of Wisconsin and has been a high school and college teacher.

24